THE COMPLETE
TO BUILD

8 FIGURE WEBSITE

FROM PLANNING TO PROFITING

BY JIM SABELLICO

Copyright © 2021 Jim Sabellico.

All rights reserved. No part of this book may be reproduced, stored, or transmitted by any means—whether auditory, graphic, mechanical, or electronic—without written permission of both publisher and author, except in the case of brief excerpts used in critical articles and reviews. Unauthorized reproduction of any part of this work is illegal and is punishable by law.

CONTENTS

Foreword v

Chapter 1   The Importance of Branding 1

Chapter 2   Defining Your Customer Avatar 7

Chapter 3   Do the Research 12

Chapter 4   Positioning Your Offer 17

Chapter 5   Content is King 22

Chapter 6   Hire an Expert 30

Chapter 7   Getting Your First Sale 37

Chapter 8   Build Your Email List 46

Chapter 9   Closing the Sale 57

Chapter 10 Climbing the Value Ladder 68

Chapter 11 Generating Traffic 74

Chapter 12 Measuring and Optimizing 83

Chapter 13 The Importance of Going Fast 90

Chapter 14 Then Go Slow and Steady 95

Chapter 15 Build a Strong Community 99

FOREWORD

Before we talk about building your eight-figure website, we should be clear about a couple of things, namely, who the heck am I, and why am I qualified to be giving you advice on this topic in the first place?

Both fair questions, so let's answer them.

My name is Jim Sabellico, I am the founder of J. Louis Technology, a digital agency based in New York that has been designing and developing websites for people since 2012, and during that time I've been a part of building precisely 21 different eight-figure websites as of the time of writing this book.

Yes sure, there are people who've been a part of bigger, or more, but for me, that's a large enough sample size for me to observe that there is a pretty clear and repeatable set of action items all 21 of those ventures have in common, and that's precisely what I'm going to outline here in this book for you.

Also, let's talk about actually achieving an 8 figure website, because somewhere in the back of your mind you are wondering if it's even possible for you. Let's stop that doubt right here, because YES IT IS.

You have everything you need to achieve that.

A very small part is the information laid out here in this book, but the biggest part is YOU.

You are more than capable of building an 8,9,10 figure business and it's already in progress, whether you realize it or not. All you need to do now is believe it, put in the work, and stay committed to it and you will see it happen.

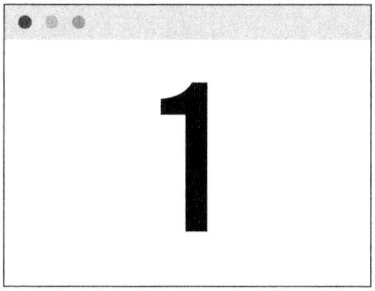

THE IMPORTANCE OF BRANDING

The Ferrari Example

Perhaps one of the best combinations of words that describes the importance of branding for any web business is what Harvard Business School Professor Stefan Thomke said in his Case Study on Ferrari. He said, "The overarching goal is to create an experience - a sensual experience."

It makes a lot of sense to think of what customers and clients will get from using a product as an experience. The truth, though, is that very few businesses know this or are trying to do it.

You can hardly mistake the Ferrari brand for another—the horse logo, red color, and the sleek, wide bodywork. But bodywork alone doesn't guarantee customer experience. The few who can afford the cars would often talk about the purr of the engines. Think of a full-grown lion lounging by you, purring as you caress his mane, an unforgettable experience. You also want customers not to forget what it felt like to find solutions while visiting your website.

YOUR PRODUCT AND CUSTOMER EXPERIENCE

The line that separates product, brand, and customer experience is a blurry one. For your online business to sell, the company must have a strong brand - one that customers recognize at a glance. Customers cannot mistake a brand's identity to associate an experience with among its peers on the internet.

Just like car lovers who value the experience of cutting edge technology and pleasure go for Ferrari, so do they seek you out in the search results when they surf the internet for whatever solution they're looking for.

To achieve customer satisfaction, you must understand precisely what your customer wants from using your product. There are a plethora of other options scattered all over the internet, so to stand out, your brand identity must be unique, its presence on the virtual shelf must be incontrovertibly attractive to clients. And a lot is riding on this.

We can go from a layman's perception of what a product is - physical, tangible articles like Coca-Cola or Pepsi drinks, or a car - to what it truly encompasses.

WHAT IS A PRODUCT?

A product refers to any article or object offered up for sale. But a product isn't only something we can touch physically; it can practically be anything from the air at the lube station, gas for cars, the truck conveying the gas; it can even be the time and skill of the gas station attendance. It can be intangible, like a service rendered by a handyman or a legal adviser.

Your product/service must address a need. When people encounter your web product or service, an unconscious debate should occur in their minds regarding their need for the product/service.

Your product must *speak*.

We can't deny the fact that products have a voice of their own. A Ferrari speaks of comfort, class, and affluence, a kid who buys a pair of converse shoes would probably think of skateboards. What's your product going to say to your chosen market? A website must communicate the goal of a product clearly to attract many more visitors; more visitors means more leads which translates to improved ROI for the business.

Your product must have a compelling identity - a memorable name.

This may remind you of a product like Coca-Cola at its conception. The original recipe by John Pemberton in 1885 contained some cocaine, an extract of the coca leaf, and that's where the product got the first half of its name, coca. The other part of the product's name, cola, is, of course, from the kola nut, a stimulant. By 1929 however, the cocaine had been wholly taken out of the Coca-Cola product. Not many people know that the name, Coca, is reminiscent of its original ingredient. It is important that when deciding on your web product, you make sure there's at least something about the name that connects with the product and that ultimately registers in the customer's mind.

Your product must be dynamic.

Why did the Coca-Cola company tweak the content of its product after a while, though? Sometimes a business must listen to its customers, and brands often do that. New corporations must be ready for this - times change, new regulations by governments, changes in public perception of a brand, and competition. These factors affect how a brand continues to do in the market. In the final analysis, every brand and product is at the mercy of these factors and more.

Your website design and product must be ready to adapt to these changes as well. For example, the Coca-Cola company had to reevaluate its product and brand to meet public perception of addictive drugs like cocaine.

The ethics of including such a substance, no matter how minute the dose in a growing brand, was a subject the executives had to reconsider. Whether you like it or not, your website would not be the only one on the virtual shelves. There will be others, probably better websites than yours. But if your brand has a name, a unique identity that sets it apart, and you are not afraid to adapt, change, to fit in a market that continues to churn products like yours out, there's a higher chance that your brand would live for centuries.

The internet is a heavily cluttered place. There are hundreds of websites featuring millions of products. When attention span is flitting at best, it is crucial to communicate the value of your web product with proper branding.

A lot about customer experience, as in the example of Ferrari, has to do with loyalty. The properties of a site's landing page - color palette, design style, logos - like Ferrari's horse logo, maybe all a customer has to see to convince themselves that they have found what they are looking for and they are where they ought to be. People react to colors and symbols more strongly. Take advantage of this in your website.

As we have seen, a business's brand is more important than you may think. It is the entire identity of your business, your company. Just like people are identified by their personalities, their brands identify companies. Social media creates stiff competition for businesses because people are exposed to new brands every day. Your business just can't afford to take branding lightly.

Now that you know what your product should look like, it is time to consider what the people who need your product look like: your customers.

DEFINING YOUR CUSTOMER AVATAR

The Vans Example.

When the California-based business was created by the Van Doren family in 1966, their business model was a simple one. They were selling directly to customers, but their target around the turn of the 1970s was narrowed down to skateboarders of the streets of sunny California.

And this trick worked tremendously.

Vans simply profiled their target customers - they called them rebels and misfits. And before long, the Vans sneakers began to enjoy cult acceptance by employing a branding strategy that focused on a section of the society of youth who considered themselves anti-establishment, the renegades. They hung in corner streets and rode skateboards.

In designing your website, you need to understand your customers and exactly what they look like.

KNOWING WHO YOUR CUSTOMERS ARE

Does this mean your website isn't for everyone? This might seem so. Consider that baby food is for babies; even though adults wouldn't necessarily die from consuming it, it certainly isn't appealing. But if there were not many babies on the market for a product meant for babies, the product can't be expected to bring in a lot of sales and money for the company.

Similarly, in designing your website, you need to understand your customer's profile. What do they look like? Where do they hang out? What is their age? What is their occupation? How much do they earn? Learning what your target customer looks like is a marketing strategy for designing your website. On the one hand, are your target customers and on the other is your product/service displayed on your website.

Once again—who are your ideal customers?

What do they want? How often do they use the internet? How often do they visit websites like the one you intend to build, and what are their interests?

The Vans company knew who their customers were - young adults. They knew where to find them - on the street. What their proclivities were - skateboarding. As you prepare to build your eight-figure website, you need to solve how your product addresses a problem that your customers experience.

Youths in the 70s found themselves in the middle of a cultural shift. Vans helped them achieve this cultural deviation and identity by providing something to unite their rebellious outlook on the establishment with a tool for this expression—skateboards—by providing them with a symbol, Vans shoes. This model may feel complicated given that the product here is a sneaker.

The logic is the same and can be applied even to your website design. Your company is working on a budget. What better way to use the funds than by identifying who the product is meant for - the customer. A good customer avatar will help the web designer properly use visual resources to target the right audience or customer. A good customer avatar sets the appropriate theme for your entire website.

Let's take, for instance, a women's fashion company looking to become an authority in their area. The color palette of the page of the website may feature the color pink prominently. You may arrive at this decision because the customers are girls between the age of 16 and 23, and the language of the content may be chic, and their role models could range from Brittany Spears, Beyonce, to Nicki Minaj.

Can you dispense with a customer avatar? No. This is a process that the product design must go through to achieve the most engagements when it is finally launched. Aside from the fact that the customer avatar helps the marketing of the products, it also maximizes sales. Already established companies do it, and if you are just starting as an online brand, you have to do it.

WHY DO YOU NEED A CUSTOMER AVATAR?

A customer avatar creates a fascinating world of customer behavior, little things such as what they eat, drink, wear, the music they listen to, where they hang out. All of these are like peering into your customer's lives. The perfect customer for your digital product is the customer that buys now, buys later, tells others about your product, and continues to buy. A customer avatar helps you anticipate changes in the customer's life, in the life cycle of their interaction with your product. With a customer avatar, you know when the time has come to change, improvise, and adapt to his new circumstances. Such customers have Customer Lifetime Values (CLV) that continue to peak. You only need to hold the iconic old-school Vans shoe in your hands to know how powerful a customer avatar is for your business, be it a startup or an old one.

You have learned that it is essential to know *precisely* who you are selling to because honestly, only by knowing exactly who your product is for can you impact your market and make sales.

Now that you know what to do, next is to do it by researching everything about your customer's avatar.

DO THE RESEARCH

Pepsi and Coca-Cola (The Cola wars).

Here we aren't focusing on the actual rivalry between the two companies, we are considering the market they fought to win, not from the customer angle, but from a research point of view. How did these two companies affect each other? And what can a budding business learn from the inside work that powered the competition?

So picture what may have happened: Coca-Cola, which debuted in 1896, started making great sales. By 1902 the cola wars had begun when Brad's Drink by Caleb Bradham was renamed Pepsi Cola. The question is, why did Bradham rename his drink and begin to make drinks that looked like Coca-Cola? Bradham waltzed around on the thin line between copyright infringement and healthy competition.

To do what the Pepsi company did requires some in-depth research into the market at the time. Coca-Cola wasn't the only drink that added cola as one of its main ingredients at the time. It was a challenging time to join a business that already seemed cramped for space. Every severe business startup must understand what such a venture involves. It requires such a deep understanding of business development which comes from research. We pick from the example of Coca-Cola and Pepsi simply how research can give a business startup an edge, or at least an elbow room in a suffocating business world.

The executives of Pepsi didn't just launch into designing a brand or product. They researched how Coca-Cola came about its brand colors, logo and how all the brand elements were helping them scale forward with customers. Then they must have sat down to scheme out a plan that takes this route—from designing bottles, colors to revolutionary advertising techniques.

One thing though, it took Pepsi a short time to level up with Coca-Cola. How did Pepsi achieve this? Your business website needs to research everything: the existing market, competitors, and your intended customer share.

HOW RESEARCH BENEFITS YOUR START-UP OR EXISTING WEBSITE

The idea is to find out what existing competition is doing right and how they're doing it. Sometimes this involves getting information on what mistakes your competitor has made and how to not make it yourself.

As a new or existing company, research would benefit your startup—before you ever design your product—in the following ways:

Discover models that are already working

The guy who made Gameboy was a worker at Nintendo, according to how the story goes. He had the fortune of working there and had seen how games were developed. He didn't have to spend sleepless nights trying to come up with the entire process. That's what often happens in the research stage. You sometimes find that you don't need to formulate a new idea for your website from scratch. In your research, you will find out how your competitors did it.

Strategically position your product.

Research can give you a more accurate picture of where you stand in the market. If you already have a test product on the market, listening to your clients may help you discover what you need to do to improve.

Adaptability

Research helps you reposition your web brand. The result of your study would show how businesses like yours are doing on the market, compared to how clients perceive your brand. This helps you adapt to the market and roll out products that represent your brand and meet your customers' expectations.

Indeed attend to client needs.

Your clients' needs are not constant. As their lives change, so do their needs. The research will help you determine when this has happened and tailor your solutions to meet these changing needs.

Research helps your business discover how clients' needs change over time so your brand can adapt. Note that new digital companies spring up every day, where you leave a weakness unattended, there you lose customers to the competition. It's a challenging world out there, but you can beat it.

Bottomline

You don't have to launch into inventing entirely new ideas. Do the research, iterate by methods your competition's process. The investigation leads to a shortcut of processes. You can cut out a lot of miles in your digital business journey just by finding out what your competition did or didn't do.

As you have seen, research helps you discover critical issues in customer behavior, product design, and market dynamics and thus avoiding mistakes that could cost your business. It enables you to evaluate your ideas, your market to see if your new vision is needed in the first place. Any time you put into research is worth it.

In the next chapter, we'll consider how to position your offer after you have gotten your facts from your research.

POSITIONING YOUR OFFER

The Apple iPhone Example.

When coming into the oversaturated world of mobile phones, Apple understood that they would have to bring something different, unique to the market. Today, the iPhone is an iconic mobile phone.

What sets Apple phones apart from the rest? It is Apple's offer.

In its copy, Apple says about the iPhone:

Every iPhone we've made—and we mean every single one—was built on the same belief. That a phone should be more than a collection of features. That, above all, a phone should be absolutely simple, beautiful, and magical to use.

Apple's offer to users and customers is a unique experience. And this was a smart move for the company because there isn't very much Apple can do with device features, apps and all, that other companies aren't doing or prepared to beat. So Apple focused instead on the customer. They asked themselves, how do we want our customers to *feel* by buying an Apple phone?

The company focused on *user experience*. What is your business offering customers?

UNDERSTANDING VALUE

Your website must offer value, a reason for its creation, a promise that this value will be delivered to the customer, and that this value will be worth every cent the customer spends in purchasing your product or services.

This value must be communicated clearly in the company's proposition. It must be delivered so that the customer can not but acknowledge that they got it.

The customer must also feel that what he has paid is not more than the value promised on the product. This value can be embodied in the whole company or its product alone, whatever rocks your boat.

For a company that's just starting, the value the customer will get from using the product must be spelled out at the point of product design and research. It helps to position your offer if you know exactly what the value of your product is.

VALUE AND MONEY

In 2019 a study found that a large percent of millennial consumers in the US would willingly pay more money for quality customer service. So less isn't always more. There is a psychology that says if the product is cheap buyers conclude its quality is too. Although this isn't the case with all products, it is a common perception.

In the earlier days of the franchises, Pepsi was perceived to be inferior to Coca-Cola. Pepsi priced theirs lower claiming that it meant you could get two Pepsi for the price of one coke.

As you build your digital product you must understand the relationship between how the value of products is perceived by customers in relation to the price of the product or service.

The value is the quality of your product or service, it is also what your customer gets from the product after paying money for it. Sometimes a customer would complain that a website is expensive if they do not get the value that you advertised at the point of sale. Conversely, a customer may consider the price low or moderate, for a web product or service if you throw in a few after-sale services that the buyer would have paid for elsewhere independent of the product.

HOW MUCH IS YOUR CUSTOMER WILLING TO PAY?

The price of a product refers to the amount in money terms that the customer is willing to pay for your product. As we have already pointed out, if the price is high, the customer would expect a high value from your web service or product. And vice versa. This helps in both the marketing and pricing of your digital product. When developing your product be sure to promote a price that is at least proportional to the value. Beware of underpricing as this may be counterproductive. Of course, you may want to target the volume of sales by pricing your product low, some do this successfully but it's rare and certainly a tricky gamble. What may save the day for your product is the utility your customers get from the purchase. In the end, your customer is willing to pay any amount for a product, provided the product has a higher value than how much money they have to pay.

Thus far, you have learned that positioning your offer is tied with the value of your product. And also how your product or service fares when placed side by side with those of your competitors. It also involves how you want your customers to perceive your product or service and the solutions you are offering. Lastly, you must know what to do to make your product deliver in the position you choose.

Now that your brand is up, your product is ready, how do you let the world know about your website or services? The answer is in the next chapter.

CONTENT IS KING

The Example of the Blog Zen habits.

The owner of this blog writes articles for daily motivation. The advice is usually so timely and true that everyone who visits the website can find something that works for them.

What makes the blog successful?

The articles are always focused on the reader, not the writer of the posts.

Reading through the posts you'll feel its pulse with the interest of the readers at the core of the writing. The words are simple and the thoughts are easy to follow. The articles are written to evoke interest, they are helpful and readers are moved to share them. The posts are not too long, most of them would take only a few minutes to read. One other thing to learn from Zen Habits is that the shorter the post, the better. And blog posts are kept short when they do not include unnecessary details, they are straight to the point and fun to read.

IMPORTANCE OF WELL-WRITTEN CONTENT

The most valuable element on any website is the content. This usually consists of written words, photos, audio, or videos about the products. The landing page usually contains copy that introduces visitors to your products and helps them become acquainted with what you have to offer.

The following are reasons why you should consider well-written content for your digital business:

Attract more sales

High-value content attracts visitors to your website because the content on your website suggests that you are an authority on the subject. A relationship is formed between you and potential customers when they can trust what they read on your website. You must leverage great content to generate leads, and in turn, sales. It is said that most prospective buyers know if they are going to do business with you from how they connect with content on your website. They need assurance that your product has value, that they can trust you to deliver what you say about your services.

When the content on your website is product-focused and customer-aware, there is a 70 percent possibility that every visitor to your site would contact you for business. Imagine what that does for your web business if 7 out of 10 people who visit your website buy your product.

Great content lasts forever

Content that is up to date on your product, principles, and popular trends continues to remain relevant every time it comes up in the search engines. Great content takes effort to put together, and it is always worth it because the resources you put into writing great content come back in many folds as profit. Knowledge of SEO helps to put great content together that will stand the test of time. Such content is written in a clear manner that provides value to the reader, and it embraces a wide range of subjects in the field which you are selling to your customer.

Great content needs continuous curation, the information you provide today may become irrelevant tomorrow, granted. But your content can remain great if you always update it, and doing this bolsters customer trust in what you have to offer. You'd be surprised that some visitors too are aware of changes, they may be checking in to see what you have to say about such reforms, and if they find you have updated such information on your website too, they leave a thumbs up, comments and even suggestions.

Here you have visitors seeking to maintain a relationship with a respected site. It's a good feeling you get when you realize that you are adding value to your customers' lives.

Attract more traffic and engagement

Quality attracts attention. As an African proverb says, people bother a fruit tree more than they do one that is just a tree.

Your website can remain just that, a website, or it can be a treasure trove of seemingly unending information. It can be disheartening to check your stats and hear the echoing silence of nothing, an indication that traffic has only been a trickle. This means your website is not showing up on the search results. This is what great content remedies. Well-written content travels around the internet, it is a journeyman. You'd be surprised to find your content in the strangest places, shared by multiple people, multiple times. That's the power of great content.

People often share content on the internet for many reasons. It may be because they found it funny, informative, educational, engaging, or even controversial. Others share stuff just because they disagree with the writer and would love to know who else shares their distaste for the content. In the process of engaging with your content, your prospects engage with your brand and this brings you closer to them.

Maximize SEO

Premium quality content gives your website strong SEO standing. The truth of the matter is if you want people to discover your website in the morass that is the internet, if you want to get high on hits, you need to understand SEO, and that is the point of it all, to be seen. This is one benefit of writing great, quality articles that incorporate SEO best practices.

You may have spent resources and huge amounts of time writing great material yet your articles cause no ripple in the vast ocean of written materials like yours. You need to understand the proper keywords to target, on-page optimization, backlinks, and many other search engine optimization tips that boost the performance of content on search engines and take advantage of this.

Well interlinked content enables website navigation.

It is easier for visitors to navigate your website, and they can find content easily that suits their taste. For example, a visitor who's interested in reading about a particular product you advertised on your website may, after reading about that product, want to discover more products that look like it. If you make proper use of internal links in your content, they are bound to find related articles on your website more easily. Moreover, it should not be difficult to find the share buttons. An impressed and satisfied visitor usually wants to share the information on Facebook, Twitter, or other social media spaces.

Strategies for Writing Great Content

Identify, Agitate and Solve.

One of the best formulas for writing content for your website and causing a huge improvement in your web business is the one where you, first, identify what the problem is, agitate that problem and then demonstrate how to solve it.

You can hardly miss with this technique and your website will begin to experience conversions more than ever before. This technique works like magic especially for sharing your blog or web posts on your social media handles. The application of this technique is endless but let's restrict ourselves to your business website.

To illustrate this formula, let's take the example of someone who wants to write a blog post on how to get more engagement on your Facebook post. Here's the sample content:

[Identify a problem]

You've written a great post but what you hear are crickets around it? Three hours after, not a single reaction?

[Agitate the problem]

Many Facebook users wish they got reactions for their posts, comments too. But it just seems like they are invisible on the timeline. They scroll through and see even posts that aren't as loaded as theirs gathering those coveted reactions like ants to sugar.

Yet, there you sit staring at the post you made three days ago gathering a pithy three likes and no comment.

[Solve the problem in a systematic process]

Here's how to get crazy reactions to your Facebook posts.

In the example above, I identified the problem which is, inability to get reactions on Facebook posts. Then I agitated this problem in the mind of the reader by blowing it up, making him feel emotional about the problem, to draw him into the issue at hand. In the final section, I provided a solution.

At the end of a post, you can encourage your reader to share your content.

If you solve one person's problem, they like what they read or watch on your website and hit the share button. The possibilities that follow this act are endless.

The point is, consistent, high quality content is a huge factor for growing your new business.

Content impacts buyer decisions more than any other form of advertising. Content propagates your brand. If you are relentless with great content, your brand will always be open to discovery at every customer touch point. Remember to let your content portray a unique voice, a style that is easily identifiable across all your distribution avenues.

But what if you have no writing skill? Find out what to do in the next chapter.

HIRE AN EXPERT

Preliminary Thoughts.

You are sitting at your table, staring at all the work you have done in preparation for building your website; you're surrounded by your team, all you have for illumination is the glare from your computers and overhead fluorescent light. You and your team are at the point where you are sure it is time to put all the results from your research into building a website. Depending on the nature of the website you will require more than your ten hands. You want to do a great job in terms of functionality, interface, and outlook. Translating everything from a mere idea into reality requires considerable effort.

How long the job will take depends on the nature of the website. It could be anything from a couple of weeks to a month or even more. You understand that you are not only after aesthetics, your strategy for building the site must align with the goal of the website. Before going to work, identify what the purpose of the site is. The goal of the site must be clear from the beginning of the project. Knowing the goal of the site gives you an idea of the scope of the work involved. You are looking at a conglomerate of pages, metadata, and other behind-the-scenes elements that will not be visible to visitors. After having a layout describing the scope of the website, you need the sitemap. With the sitemap on hand, you can determine how the elements that make up the website would all complement each other.

The website is like a car's engine, content is like gas that makes it move. Your website is a big hunk of hardware without content. Bearing the goal of the website in mind, and also letting search engine optimization (SEO) be your guide, you will need preliminary content for the new site. What follows are the visuals for the website, style tiles, element collages, and mood boards, all the little things that make the whole.

You are done with the heavy parts of the project, it is time to test it. This would involve checking in on the website from different devices to see how web pages flow from one to the other, how the colors match, and if the links work properly. Once you are satisfied with the result of your work, then it is time to launch.

You have to first figure out how you want the world to know about the website. Are you running free or paid adverts on social media or simply using an existing email list? Much would depend on the goal of the website and the budget.

EXECUTION OF THE PROJECT: HIRE EXPERTS.

Now that you know most of what is involved in doing the job; you probably have a team of people you work with, or it could simply be you alone hacking it in the world of web designing as a beginner. Most beginners are tempted to assume every single responsibility in the project for reasons that range from limited resources to confidence in their abilities. You are not an expert at everything, and even if you do know how to do it all, there are more advantages to hiring experts than trying to do every task by yourself.

Here are some reasons why you need to hire experts:

You are not a single tree.

Tree experts often speak of the interconnection of tree roots in forests - basically, as trees grow their roots become entangled underground and because of this they each become stronger and sturdier than they normally would be on their own.

This is much the same with your eight-figure website, you can not do it all by yourself. You need other people's input in your projects, they see things you might miss and in ways that may not occur to you. Of course, there would be stuff you are personally best at, however, that's only related to your product or the service you render. There will be other aspects you need experts for, do not be afraid or let pride hold you back from requesting assistance. You may find the professional aspect of your business easier to handle while you hire an expert to handle your web designing concerns.

Opportunity to build a team

The human race thrives on this interconnectivity where we all come together to accomplish a task. When you hire experts, you form new relationships with people, the next time you need to work on another web design project you know who to call. Of course, business is kept in its place but a team of friends working together is far more refreshing than with strangers. A team consists of people who already understand each other.

A network of experts

Having one expert in your business can open a world of other experts, as referrals, and soon what you have is a network of experts. This has invaluable effects on your business. As an example, a professional web designer knows a reliable SEO expert if you need to work with one, and so on.

Running a business is not an easy feat, but having a network of people you can trust to deliver on projects or components of it is something to cherish and value.

Save time

You save time when you hire experts; the time it takes to get jobs done as it should be; the time it takes to smash your competitor's website; the time it takes for your business to grow online. Having experts working with you shrinks growth time from ten years to about half of that if you have experts around you to leverage. And this is one of the most important pleasures you derive from working with experts, you get to leverage their skill to boost your web business while you focus on other parts of your business which can help increase your ROI. You are leveraging your hired expert's years of experience, and all the people he or she knows.

You save money too

Hiring experts causes a reduction of risks. They have experience, you can depend on them to work under less supervision, they can help shortcut certain processes thereby reducing overall cost for you. Many beginners avoid experts because they feel it costs more to hire them . But it turns out to be more expensive to hire a hack. Your business and reputation are at stake, you may lose big clients when these hacks deliver shoddy jobs on your behalf. You can't trust an amateur to point out the quality in an area of your business where you are less proficient but an expert would help you with that.

YOUR RELATIONSHIP WITH EXPERTS YOU HIRE

Working with people on a project that means this much to you can be challenging. You have a vision for the overall movement of your business, and you have a specific picture in your head for each particular project, and not all who work with you get your drift all the time. Interests clash, and opinions differ. It takes great self-control to be calm in situations where hired experts diverge in their opinion.

You have to listen to the experts

One of the things you come to understand as you work with a team is learning when to be quiet and listen to experts, and when to speak. It makes sense to listen because when it comes with the job of the hired expert to guide you in areas where you are not so proficient. One of the ways to achieve balance is to remember that your product must always advocate your brand. In your meetings with your team, always highlight this: how does going in this direction further the brand?

Be a good listener, do not be too quick to discard their input. You have web designers and developers working with you - value their experience. They have worked on similar projects so they likely know your project's outcome. Note that they are working on your project based on the outcome of their research. If they tell you that a particular theme is what appeals to your audience but you have a preference for another theme, you need to listen to their professional perspective as in the long run you would find their advice invaluable.

So, don't be the business owner that moves faster than their shadow. It is true you are the visioneer but then again your strength may not be in web designing. Let the professionals handle all the heavy lifting that comes with designing your eight-figure website.

When hiring experts, be sure to look into their history. Find out who they've worked for, consider testimonials from previous clients, check out their education. Look into their organizations, if they belong to any. Read up their articles if they've written any, check their photos to know who they know (since you'd be benefiting from their contacts). Find out if they've collaborated with other experts and how such associations turned out. Make sure to engage the experts before hiring them; via their blog posts, video calls, emails, and other means in order to establish some familiarity and understanding.

GETTING YOUR FIRST SALE

The Tommee Tippee Example

Tommee Tippee is a child care brand that is based in the UK. It is the fifth-largest child care company in the world popular for its unique spill-proof cups. Even though the company was originally founded in the US, there came a time after the company was sold that it had to break into the US market again. To get mother's—who were the target market—to start buying the product, Tommee Tippee did something unusual, they took child care advice considered rubbish and printed them on baby wipes. So moms would be wiping literal poop with those pieces of bad advice. It was a neat way to get people to love the brand. It was a campaign to draw attention to the brand at launch.

What the company did can be broken down into a simple logic: they took nursing mothers' needs and created an experience around them.

Nursing mothers need wipes for their babies. And there already existed other products in the market; Tommee Tippee simply printed the advice from parenting help books that they believe mothers found annoying and unhelpful on their wipes. And it was a hit.

Here's the takeaway from this: Launch your web product drawing attention to the experience your customers will get from using the product or service.

Let's take another example: NÜTRL VODKA SODA. The company was trying to break into the beverage market but with a product unlike most in the market. The problem was that people found it hard to believe that the soda contained only Nütrl vodka, carbonated water, and dashes of natural lemon juice. How does the company convince customers that their product was healthier than wines and beers that contained unhealthy additives?

The company used 30-second videos featuring people "breaking up" with wine, 15 seconds radio spots, and banner ads for advertisement. They ran co-op Facebook ads with retailers that helped increase awareness and sales.

Here's the takeaway here: Launching your product will take careful planning and forethought. These examples show that you are allowed to get creative.

THINK BIG, START SMALL: THE LAUNCH

Your first big sale from your website is probably still down the road, but we are not even thinking that far yet. Small steps amount to big ones. Your first launch doesn't necessarily have to make the national news (it's okay if you have the finance to make the evening news).

Your website launch has to be something that sticks on people's minds for a long time; it has to make an impression. Before you ever think of making a sale, you first promote your website to a target audience. Your launch must be deliberate and decisive.

Follow these steps to launch your product:

Test the product

No matter how great your product or how ingenious you believe it is, it is important not to list it on your site right away. You can look for where your target audience hangs out - Facebook groups, Linkedin groups, Quora forum, Reddit, and any social media network you can find your target audience.

You could ask members to indicate interest in using a trial version of your web product. You need their feedback on how your product works. You'd be surprised by their response too, things you overlooked could be spotted by test users. It is far better for this select group of users to find the faults in your product than for the general public to use the product once, leave terrible reviews that would mar the prospect of the product for life.

For example, consider something that happened in the African country Nigeria in 2021. The microblogging site Twitter was banned by the government of that country when twitter deleted the tweets of the president of Nigeria. A Nigerian quickly took advantage of the ban and released his version of Twitter called Crowe. The app gathered reviews that swung from horrible to hilarious on Google's play store. Users complained of glitches and endless technical faults, leading to its deletion from the play store. Do not rush to launch before testing the web service you want to promote.

Use Influencers

It has become common practice for companies, especially big ones, to target influencers when pushing out new products. No matter how great your product is, if you post it on your website or social media pages alone, you are unlikely to make sales. As a startup, you need the exposure that influencers can give your brand. This is one effective way to launch your product or website.

If it's a new product, send a sample to influencers on a list you have made, let them test it. It could also be other brand advocates of products in your niche. Make a list of famous bloggers, popular social media figures, who's-who who customers have bought your products in the past if any. Send out free samples to them asking for reviews - expect most of them to be positive. In return for negative reviews, ask for suggestions and use them, then send the products back for review again. This is all part of your product launch when satisfied members of your test group post about your product on their social media pages or blogs.

Do not lose sight of the purpose of this idea which is to create awareness, a buzz. The excitement from your test members can be infectious for the general public. This could cost some money. But it would be money well spent.

Get Your Team Involved

Your team is a part of your launch, but your product launch may run aground if they are not as excited as you are. Assign mini-projects, have them go over the process with you in detail so that everyone knows what is expected of them. A product launch can happen in a day; the launch can also be protracted, a campaign that goes on over time. Each member of your team—product manager, sales representatives—should be provided with resources needed to help them fulfill their responsibilities.

Create a timetable for the launch

It is easy to get carried away with a particular wing of the launch and lose sight of an equally important part of the whole. This is why you need a proper, clearly marked schedule, perhaps a written one on a whiteboard where everyone on your team sees it. Every step is marked out as the launch progresses. Launching a new web product can be daunting; your head swirls with so many details, plus the anxiety of doing everything right can make you forget the important stuff. Your schedule or timetable board can help you keep track of your launch process.

Every smart entrepreneur knows how important a schedule is. It reflects positively on your company and finally on your end product. Clients and prospective buyers tell from how you administer your website that your business is run by a solid schedule and that you stick by it. It reflects on how you use time too, and your team respects you for this. They'll take you seriously because you take your business seriously. Create a timetable for your launch and stick to it.

They say something written down is sealed on the mind and is hardly ever forgotten. Write your entire goal and get your team to familiarize themselves with it.

What you should write includes how many units of your product you wish to sell in how many days, weeks, or months.

Your list should include how you want to achieve this number of sales.

Write the name of each blogger, influencer, friend, the family members you want to be involved in this campaign, and the nature of their involvement.

This guides the language of your memos; it also helps you project how much you expect each of them to do.

Give room for flexibility, review your list as you go, and make amendments to fit rising contingencies. Flexibility helps decide when to schedule your launch too.

Some products are seasonal. A proper schedule helps you avoid getting ahead of yourself in your excitement to get your products out there.

Diversify Your Marketing Channels

We live in an age when there are diverse ways to get your product in the face of prospective customers. There are more ways to reach people than twenty years ago when salesmen had to knock on people's doors from state to state advertising their products. Today, you have the unique opportunity like never before to tell people about your product through social media channels: Google Ads, telegram channels, Facebook ads and dedicated pages, Twitter, email lists, TV advertising, radio, and many more. Your options are countless, and you are allowed to be creative with them. Do not restrict yourself to a single channel; your audience is waiting everywhere.

Take advantage of folks on your contact list - family, friends, and acquaintances. Directly share links to your website, or invite them to read articles you think they'd find valuable. Share links to your site on your Facebook page and group.

Use fun ways to encourage engagement.

Ask visitors to sign up to receive newsletters or to drop comments to share their suggestions. Encourage them to use the share button to spread the word.

The Tommee Tippee company focused on user experience, which is one of the best ways to attract patronage to a new product since there's an array of products like yours on the internet. Highlight the uniqueness of your product and why your customers need it.

Nütrl vodka soda company understood that most customers will not take the company's word for it. Most doubted that the product contained what was promised. Hence, instead of convincing the public to buy their drink, they convinced them to stop drinking wine and beer. The short videos focused on "breaking up" with beer and wine, pricking on the buyer's inner guilt of consuming something that harms their health.

Family and friends are the most difficult to convince sometimes. This is why the method outlined above works fine in most cases. When most see why they've been doing isn't the best, they are more likely to opt for the alternative you provide. Your web solutions will attract customers if they know it doesn't only solve their problems, it also saves them money.

In this chapter, we showed that getting your very first sale is a massive milestone in your new business. It takes some time and focus to achieve, but the point of it all is simple: get people to see your website. If you can get consistent traffic to your website, you land that first sale in no time. So knowing what to focus on makes all the difference. Tweaking your website every which way may be a waste of time. Instead, concentrate right now on traffic.

One of the most important steps towards getting more sales will be discussed in the next chapter.

BUILD YOUR EMAIL LIST

You only need to open your email box to find out what an email list is: because you are probably on several companies' mailing lists. Those innocuous emails that keep coming in, that your mailbox cached under promotions, yes, those.

Open one of them and see how it is all specially addressed to you. It is like a letter from a buddy out of town who's writing to check on you, asking to know if you've visited their website recently and seen the latest product or service from them. They want to let you know this new product was designed with you in mind and they want you to check it. There's a link in the body of the email that directs you to the website to either read or directly purchase the new product or simply just add it to your cart. Everyone that has a personal email has this section in their email box filled with these messages. You may have even bought a product before because one of these emails suggested you do.

Your website is losing out on conversion if you don't have an email list.

WHY HAVE AN EMAIL LIST

You are getting started in your website business, your launch is well underway, and you have made some sales. Hopefully you gathered the emails of clients and visitors to your website during your launch, this is what constitutes your email list. You can build your email list through Call To Action buttons (CTA) on all the landing pages, with a promise to deliver newsletters to your visitors, or some other type of 'bait'.

Emails still have good conversion rates.

Emails are for the most part free to send and free to receive, and almost everyone checks their emails every day, emails are easily accessible on mobile phones and computers, and they are private. All of these characteristics make emails one of the very best tools for your website business. Big businesses like Amazon do this all the time and enjoy huge conversions for profit. Pop-Ups on your landing pages request visitors' emails so they can receive offers when a new product is available. An automated mailing list sends new product notifications, and visitors who don't buy the first time can buy later. They remain tethered to your website as potential customers for as long as your business continues to exist. It is a constant and regular cycle of offer notifications.

Email lists generate traffic for your website and business.

The internet is an ocean of websites offering a plethora of things. It is not likely that a visitor who was on your website today will be back tomorrow except if they have been invited, especially by your email. Attention spans have painfully reduced with too many distractions on the internet. Having an email list helps generate constant traffic to your website. Carefully worded emails are important.

Corey Dilley of Unbounce says, "Email marketing consistently generates 80-90% of our landing page traffic when we launch a new campaign, piece of content, or product feature." Once again, the higher your traffic, the higher your conversions.

An email list connects you with your audience.

There is something peculiar happening when a visitor clicks on your link and spends time on your website. They are looking for something, a product, an article discussing the solution to their problem. If a hundred visitors come to your website, they have to be yours. You can't let the chance for a bond, an interaction, go to waste. An email personalizes this meeting between your website, business, and the visitor. When you get an email from a visitor, it gives you a critical opportunity to know who your visitor is and what products to sell to them.

An email list protects and promotes your business.

To help people find your website or business on the internet, you do all this research to get past the Google algorithm and get to your customers. But you can't always get it right. And sometimes, you are penalized by Google without even knowing what you did wrong and may experience a low in traffic. Here's where the email list that you have protects your business. People on your list—both old and new customers or clients—continue to get offers from you no matter what. Anyone who voluntarily gives you their email is telling you they are ready to receive offers from you; they are telling you they are prepared to read more articles on your website, so you have an endless, inexhaustible opportunity to promote your product or website to them.

With emails, you don't worry about restrictions.

You read that right. Emails are that golden. No middlemen or restrictions on how many times a week or how many products, or how many people you can send emails to. You often wonder what's happening to your Facebook or Twitter efforts when your engagements are low. Those platforms often restrict how many people your posts reach to make you pay for ads. With emails, as long as the customer has permitted you to send them emails, your marketing is on a constant roll. The sweet thing about email lists is that people's connection to them is different than that of Facebook or Twitter. With other media, posts have no separate ownership; they are just there for anyone to see. But when customers receive an email, they know it is addressed to them personally; their names are on it. The email lands in their inbox; they can read it anytime they want and how many times they want.

An email list gives you reach

Reach is a coveted thing among website owners. And businesses that hope to make unceasing sales must worry about it. Your product will remain on the shelf where it would gather dust and cobwebs without reaching customers. Your website will have crickets screaming there like quiet nighttime in movies if only a handful of people click your links once every week. It isn't quite a predicament if you have an email list and you use it.

True, reach remains a thing to contend with in the virtual world. Less than three percent of those on your friend list on Facebook see your posts, and so it is with other social media like Twitter. Your chances are far higher with emails. More than 70% of emails get opened and read by recipients. Yes, quite a few land in the spam folder and may never get to be read. But some folks prowl their email boxes, even their spam folder to see what's waiting there (I'm one of them).

The point is your email will be opened and read. Make sure your content is well written, make it interesting. Even if the first couple of emails wind up in the spam folder, you can be sure that if the recipient finds the content useful they will start or move your email to the primary inbox.

HOW TO BUILD YOUR EMAIL LIST

Many people consider email marketing old school. They either find it strenuous or archaic. This does not diminish that it is still one of the best ways to market your product or web business. Here are a few strategies to begin growing your email list:

Plan and know your target audience

Depending on what your product is, or the niche of your website, you need to take some time to plan out who your target audience is and where you are likely to find them. Furthermore, you need to understand beforehand what sort of content is appropriate for that audience.

Following this, you need to decide the bait that you can use to attract your leads. The bait could be anything from specific giveaways—free eBooks, cheat sheets and swipe files, Whatever you think your audience would consider valuable enough to let you have their email.

Use signup forms on your website

Put your sidebar, footer, and about page to effective use. Be clear and straight to the point with the request for emails. Instead of saying, "SIGN UP HERE, or SUBSCRIBE HERE," be more deliberate and direct. Say something like, "ENTER YOUR EMAIL ADDRESS HERE TO RECEIVE UPDATES ON NEW PRODUCTS, PROMOTIONS, AND SPECIAL OFFERS."

Personalize your emails

Own your email list, be passionate and friendly when you write. Personalize the email by using the recipient's name, be conversational but not too informal. Let them know you won't sell their emails to third parties and that you value their privacy. Create an autoresponder series so that new subscribers can easily join the list creating new engagement. How many emails per month should you send out? Well, that depends on a few factors like, how often do you come up with new products? How much of a prolific writer are you? Do you have someone on your staff who manages these communications? Some savvy marketers suggest more than once a month. If you have a robust email list you may want to keep this communication to a monthly one.

One thing is for certain, don't be afraid to USE YOUR LIST. Those people signed up to be marketed to, so market to them, they don't do you any good if you never send them anything.

Optimize your emails for mobile phones

The majority of people are on the move, they want to check their email on the train, on their flight, and while sitting on the commode. They want to keep up with their life as fast as possible. It would be a waste if your email arrives and the recipient is unable to read it on their mobile phone because it doesn't open properly. Early in 2021, it was found that about 46% of all emails were opened via mobile. The numbers will climb as more people favor mobile apps and use the internet on their mobile phones.

Whatever strategy you are using, make sure to keep track of how these emails translate to profits for your business, and on how they drive engagement for your website. The more turnover for your efforts you see the higher the morale for your business.

BENEFITS OF AN EMAIL LIST

It is personal

As already mentioned, every email you send out arrives in the personal email box of the recipient. And if it's not in their spam folder, they'd almost always open it and find what new product or blog post you have prepared for them. They find the language personal too as you address them by their name.

Emails are more suited for business.

And this is the truth. Emails are formal, it is the first choice for most businesses. While people prefer to carry out other interactions on other social media places like Facebook Messenger and WhatsApp, they prefer to exchange business ideas, prices, and products using email. Nothing beats an email list for budding businesses.

Formal intimacy.

It is both formal and intimate at the same time and this is what makes emails special. You can address your customers' needs, answering their questions while keeping the tone intimate. Both parties can exchange emails in this private space without feeling that they are stepping over personal boundaries.

Emails can be easily targeted.

Using email marketing software can help you send emails in groups, emails that are targeted to specific clients, dealing with specific issues. It makes engaging with your customers easy and in short, precise language be able to answer their questions and update them about new web products or services.

Your contact book.

As I noted somewhere earlier, followers of your business on social media aren't yours, they belong to Facebook, Twitter, and Instagram because those social mediums connect you both, and they can easily disconnect you as well, especially if their policies suddenly change. Your reach is reduced, can be tampered with, and all not to your favor. But your email list is yours; you collected the emails yourself. There are no middlemen with powers to take them away at a whim.

Emails will always be here.

More than half of the population of the world has at least an email. And the number is expected to continue to climb in the future. Emails are not going anywhere. Everyone continues to need one, even to register on social media. Email marketing will always be here, so continue to add subscribers and cash out.

High conversion rates.

Emails help you convert those visitors to your websites into buyers faster. If you have a great website business and you have an email list, send out targeted emails and watch your clicks grow. It is easier to convert those emails to sales than any other marketing technique.

Your email list serves the purpose of providing a perpetual pool of leads, a ready-made group for testing new products and providing feedback on satisfaction. You can track how they interact with your website utilizing your email list, or how they interact with your customer care.

You may be tempted to buy email subscribers. Please don't. Doing this hurts your brand, wasting both your time and your potential customers' own. Your email will end up in the spam folders. Unsolicited messages only give your brand a bad image. Don't ask for too many details when building your email list. Offer strong incentives. Make sure your new subscribers get a welcome mail first before proceeding to other matters. Always ask for feedback.

Now that your email list is running, leads are coming in. How do you make them buy your web services? Learn about closing sales in the next chapter.

CLOSING THE SALE

Grant Cardone says, "In selling you are seeking an agreement. Your customer is almost always distrustful and uncertain, not about you, but themselves. Most salespeople think selling is about gaining trust, but in reality, selling is about getting the customer to trust themselves enough to take action and close—which often takes flexibility. Learn to *close* the sale, not just *make* a sale."

WHAT DOES IT MEAN TO CLOSE A SALE?

Charles Dickens and other 19th century writers of the English language used the term *close* concerning bargains and transactions. It became popular with real estate deals where the seller of a house is said to have closed a sale the moment the buyer pays the amount in money for the house and takes possession of the property. It is now a general term in marketing to mean achieving the outcome which is a sale. It can also mean the moment when a prospect, a buyer makes the purchase.

If your website is new on the market, it can be intimidating to encounter a buyer who is reluctant to make a purchase even though from all indications, the buyer desires the product or service. This is why you must learn how to initiate a purchase. A reluctance on your part to make this happen opens you up for a painful rejection. Even as the phrase suggests, it is the salesperson who's closing the sale, not the buyer. The salesperson is the one instigating the action of purchase. Some buyers find themselves floating in that nebulous place between making the decision to shell out the cash and receiving the product. You need to be alert to know when this is happening.

However, it doesn't have to be a daunting exercise. And the process can be simple. You only need to be confident that you have done your work properly from the early stage of the interaction with the prospect.

BEFORE YOU EVER GET TO CLOSING THE SALE

First, you have to make a sales presentation. Your sales presentation depends much on the nature of your product or services. Some products require that the buyer and seller are physically present in a room. Nowadays, a product's SEO landing page is an avenue for the prospect to encounter the product or service. This page creatively presents the offer and educates the prospect on the benefit of acquiring the product. It could be a simpler process that involves a prospect from your email list who reaches out and asks for more information about a product or service. This exchange may take a few days after which a prospect makes a purchase. Experts say no one should go into any business—even website business—without learning how to market and sell.

The following tips provide an idea for all situations of sales presentation.

Keep it simple.

Your presentation should be short. Use simple language that evokes curiosity in what you have in store. Prick at the interest of your listeners. Shroud your beginning in some mystery to keep your listeners wanting more, use anticipation to keep them glued to you until the big reveal. Do this and the whole process doesn't feel like you are simply presenting a dissertation.

Use storytelling.

The best salespersons use storytelling techniques when presenting their pitches. Listen to an audio version of a book by your favorite novelist, if you have one. See how they use tone, pitch, and how they enunciate. Like when telling a story, use imaginary characters that your listeners can relate to and highlight how the web product you are pitching on helped this character. Make sure to give this character life, a description that your audience can relate to.

Have deep insights into your listeners.

What are their worries and doubts, their pains? How can your product solve these problems? You should have a dossier on each of your listeners and go over them repeatedly to have a complete grip on their realities. When presenting, you can build the fictional character's life around the insights you have on your audience. This helps the presentation to resonate with your listeners, making a sale easier to achieve because they're already oiled for it.

It is not a lecture.

Yes, always remind yourself that it isn't a lecture. And your audience are not students. They are your prospects. They will not take everything you say hook, line, and sinker. You'd want them to accept your product or service wholeheartedly and that only happens in the true sense if they know for certain that your product will solve their problems. So make the presentation conversational; ask questions, and encourage them to ask theirs too. And be sure to answer their questions.

Get to the point.

Don't ramble on about a point, over-flogging it. Know everything about your product or service, and everything about how it can help your prospect. Include a frequently asked questions section and, be sure to provide short answers. Avoid going off point, and when it's your audience who happens to do that, gently stir the conversation back on track. Avoid interrupting or arguing with your customer, especially if you're making a pitch with a single client.

Be a showman.

Ask yourself what you can do to help you incorporate some showmanship in your presentation, something dramatic at the opening of your presentation. You do not just appear and pour words into the air, you can make use of little props to describe the meat of your point which is: your audience needs to buy your product. It could be a smart use of colors, diagrams, or the likes. Incorporate whiteboards or flip arts, show numbers, draw little figures that explain your points.

Have confidence in your product.

If you don't exude passion for your product how do you convince your audience to make a purchase? Avoid being too emotional about the sale, in particular, that may put your audience on edge. Be passionate about the product as a solution to your audience's pains. Be confident in the power of the product, your audience will see it and want to buy. You are on your way to closing the sale.

QUESTIONS TO ASK YOUR PROSPECTS THAT COULD PROPEL SALES

After the presentation, the following questions lead the prospect on to make a purchase:

DO YOU HAVE ANY QUESTIONS?

This is the question you ask after your presentation. From here you can tell if your prospect will make the purchase and if you'd close the sale. The prospect would usually ask his questions. You'd make more clarifications. As you do, watch for signs that the prospect understands the answers you provide.

WHAT DO YOU NEED TO MOVE FORWARD?

You ask this when the major questions have been answered, and what you consider as obstacles are out of the way. Occasionally a prospect may say something vague like, "Well, I don't know. I think I might have to give all of this some thinking over." This doesn't have to spell trouble. One thing you must not do is panic. Remain professional.

Humans are dynamic beings. Our emotions are constantly changing on a decision especially when we have options to choose from. As you may have learned, most people's decision to purchase products is fueled by their emotions, not logic. Don't force your product down your prospect's throat.

The following are some further effective questions to ask:

What are your long-term or short-term goals?

You continue to show interest in his goals. Perhaps he doesn't see your product or service being of help to him at the moment, but how about in the future? Outline how he could be making a great decision to buy in the future. Show him how you both can work together to make his goals come to fruition.

What's holding you back from achieving these goals?

Prospects may often be less open about their failures except if they fully trust you. But if they open up to you, be sure to treat what they say confidentially. Be respectful. Ask if you can assist them to achieve these goals.

What is your (or company's) decision process like?

This is a very vital question to ask. You may be expecting a close right after the presentation, but your prospect may be looking to get back to the chain of command in his company. Standing right at the door, befuddled by your prospects' reluctance, but he may be thinking of asking for his wife's thoughts on the product. You may be getting ahead of your prospects' decision-making machine.

Is there a particular outcome you are looking for with this product or service?

Most times the answer is yes. And it could be well outside your projections and could be something your presentation omitted. But don't feel bad about this. The answer you get for this question goes in your archive of possible considerations for other presentations. You can still close this sale.

Is anyone else involved in this purchasing decision, who are they?

As we have seen before, for some companies, there is a chain of command or a superior whom the prospect has to report to before he can make a purchase, and this may constitute the reasons for his reluctance. Knowing who else is involved in the purchase can help you determine if you may need a second presentation or not.

The most important thing is that your prospect buys what they want and need. Never try to push a prospect into buying your product. They should buy of their own volition.

Strategies of Closing a Sale

How you close the sale depends on the product, the prospect, and his circumstances. The following are basic ways to close a sale:

The Assumptive Close: As the word suggests, you close the sale yourself by assuming that the buyer is about to pay. Call it a power of suggestion when suddenly the prospect says, 'oh yes,' and he signs the check over. Well, maybe not that easy but the point is clear. If it's a piece of cloth, you ask, "The sequined one or the lace?"

If it's kitchen equipment you say, "Our trucks are available to make deliveries, Mondays to Friday. What day would it be?"

The question suggests that the buyer has already made his decision to buy the product or services. Without being unduly pushy, you put the prospect in the frame of mind to buy, he likely forgets about whatever reservations he has about buying and begins to think about cash or check.

The Time Limit Close: This one is the antidote for the poisonous and famous rejection, "I'd like to think about it first." When a prospect wants to reject your offer, they almost always use this one. Even when you feel your heart sink to the bottom of your belly, man up and don't show how devastated you are. Breathe, give him a pleasant smile—don't flinch in your posture—and reply, "Good, I understand you'd want to think it over. However, I want you to know this particular model of the product is already in short supply as it's hot on the market now. I'd hate for it to be out of stock when you are ready to buy."

Or something along this line. Or you may say, "If you make a purchase now you'd be eligible for a ten percent discount…"

Including this in your offer page will make him begin to think that he would be losing something by not buying the product immediately. He may even begin to think his reason for not buying isn't that important after all.

The Custom Close: With the custom close you are bringing into play information you have gathered about the prospect and his preferences; the color specifications, size, the type, and what their budget can cover. You simply include this in your offer page on your website, reminding the prospect of what he asked for in the following manner, "You want a module of the fan that is white, five feet in height, five hours battery life after a full charge and does not cost more than $220. Is there anything else you want along with it?"

If they click, yes, send them to the checkout page. If they decide not to pay, provide an alternative item which they would be interested in buying for a cheaper amount.

What we have discussed are general ways of closing sales. Interestingly though, the virtual space is now a growing sales environment. Many sales people find it difficult to close sales online, they want to meet face to face because they are more confident when they shake hands physically. But if you familiarize yourself with the latest technologies, you can get comfortable as well online. But the same principles apply as I have said before. Learn to listen to your prospect. Some prospects do prefer to meet online, they love the anonymity. Don't force a face to face meeting. In fact what better place to provide proof that your web solution is the best than online? If you learn how to close sales online, it boosts customer confidence in your product.

As a business owner, one of your important goals is to close sales. What happens though after closing the sale? Do you keep seeking out new buyers or do you follow up with former customers? In the next chapter we learn one of the ways you can make customers continue to maintain a flow of patronage.

CLIMBING THE VALUE LADDER

The Example of The Masterclass Folks.

You have probably encountered them on social media like Facebook offering a masterclass for learning how to code, for writers, singers, craftsmen, and the likes. They advertise with high-quality videos in which they make their pitch, at the bottom of the video is a tab to click if you are interested in knowing more. You are taken to their website where there's a box to click, at the end of which a free offer is waiting for you. You are usually blown away by the value of the free stuff. You want to join the masterclass as soon as possible. The cost of the class isn't a hindrance because a taste of the free stuff suggests something of even higher value is in the offing.

What you don't know as a customer or prospect is you have been *upsold*. And we have numerous examples of this model in today's business world. This is a simple example to show what *upselling* is. Easing a prospect into your value ladder by giving this value out in bits.

There's yet a lot of people in business who are not upselling and don't have a value ladder for their business. They are leaving a lot of money out on the table. Are you leaving money on the table in your web business? A value ladder model will help you rake in as much sales as there are in the market for your website product or services.

WHAT IS A VALUE LADDER?

A simple definition says a value ladder is a range of products and services that are planned to increase in value and price. It means that your product isn't just one premium product or service sold at $500. Your products are valued from free to the next one which is $20, $50, $70, $90, $120, and up the prices go, each with its value until the final price, the premium product of $500.

WHY IS A VALUE LADDER GREAT FOR YOUR WEBSITE BUSINESS?

Value ladders are great for your business because it is easier to get an old customer to buy more from you than to get a new one to do so. An old customer would move up the value chain of your business to buy more while you're still trying to convince a new one to get on your presentation. It costs less to sell to an old customer than to a new one. With a value ladder, you can ensure that someone who has bought from you before can buy again, and continue to do so. Every customer on your list has a lifetime value, a value ladder helps your business maximize and utilize this lifetime value.

HOW DO YOU USE THE VALUE LADDER IN AN ONLINE BUSINESS?

It is my opinion that the people who enjoy using the value ladder system most are online businesses. Online businesses are most suited for the value ladder because most of them use a sales funnel.

The first level in the value ladder is free or really low barrier to entry. The visitor searches Google and finds your website in the search results, he clicks and lands on your site. He clicks on a blog post perhaps, or on a product that is advertised there. A popup appears that requests for his email so he can receive a free coupon. He drops his email and from here he finds himself on your email list.

Perhaps he receives his free coupon or maybe a free ebook. He reads and finds it very valuable. He receives more emails asking him to check out another eBook on web designing that costs him a token, say, $14 plus free shipping.

He opts-in and makes this purchase after some days. This customer has gone up the value ladder two rungs—first, it was a free eBook, now he has further purchased a $14 product. Next, you send him another web product that you believe he would love to read in his journey to becoming proficient at web designing, so maybe now you are selling him a three-day course or software that would cost him $25. He quickly makes this purchase because all along he's been getting more value than what he's paying. This fine customer and salesperson relationship continues over a period until he buys the final course or software—perhaps for pros—which costs $200.

That customer has climbed the value ladder to the point of purchasing your premium product. Consider this: would the prospect have purchased the premium product of $200 if that had been the only product on sale from the beginning?

Not likely. Maybe 1 out of every 10 visitors to your website would have purchased that product or service without the value ladder.

So instead of having people make a small purchase or a large one that is only a one-off, online businesses build an email list that allows them to utilize the lifespan of a customer's value. Prospects aren't always truthful about how much they intend to spend, whether when they appear physically at your shop, or when you exchange emails online. They most often reduce how much they are willing to spend for the value of your product. Instead of targeting a lump sum, a business can break this value into small bits beginning with the free stuff. But make sure the fee stuff has value.

This is how you upsell your customers. Upselling is a sales technique where a seller invites a buyer to progressively buy more expensive items, upgrades of the item, or add-ons. It involves showing the customer more products while the prices continue to go higher.

CROSS-SELLING IS DIFFERENT FROM UPSELLING.

While upselling refers to a technique where an upgrade of a product that a customer has bought before is promoted, cross-selling is different.

Cross-selling is commonly practiced by people like financial advisors. An example is where an income tax officer offers investment or insurance products to his tax client. You see that the seller is promoting something entirely outside his area of expertise, but related to what you're already buying.

Cross-selling may lead to a lot of profits for the seller, but it is a potentially problematic technique especially if the seller lacks requisite knowledge of the field. If a digital marketer is going to cross-sell his client he must do well to understand the product properly before promoting it. Otherwise, this may lead to losing the trust of the customer when they find they have been sold a product that doesn't meet their needs.

How do you know what to upsell a customer?

This is one of the functions of an email list as discussed earlier. In the course of exchanging emails, you get to know what interests the prospect, how they feel about certain products. When you send an email promoting products, whenever they make a purchase you can tell where their interest lies and then follow up with an upgrade in their interest but with a slightly higher price.

Design your own value ladder by understanding the nature of your market and what your competition is doing. Then you need to identify the core of your offer, the main value of your product, what it has to offer that no other product does as well. You also need a hook—your customer proposition—the thing about your product that will hold your prospect. Your free offer must be valuable enough to draw and hold your customers loyalty. Lastly, focus on customer lifetime value, and you have to be deliberate about maximizing your profit.

To maximize profit in your web business you need traffic and more traffic. How can you get them? Let's find out in the next chapter.

GENERATING TRAFFIC

Every online business thrives on traffic, without it a business can not hope to get customers. Without customers, your website business suffers. This is why businesses with online presence spend huge budgets on traffic. Writers are employed, SEO experts, social media managers too, and it's a field day for everyone involved. Millions of characters of contents are created and the internet is an ocean of written words, images, and videos. All for one purpose—traffic. Why should you be concerned about traffic for your web business?

WHY TRAFFIC IS IMPORTANT FOR YOUR BUSINESS

It is easy to think of traffic and then conclude that it only translates to more money. That is a narrow conclusion. Traffic doesn't only bring more revenue. It also means more expansion for your business, growth, and development of more products. When your traffic grows, the demand for your product is also diversified. Hence you are not just open to more revenue, but the value and reach of your product are affected. The plurality of visors all looking for different solutions makes it difficult to quantify traffic in terms of money alone.

Consider the reasons why traffic is the lifeblood of business and important for your website:

Traffic leads to conversion of numbers.

The more visitors you drive to your website the more customers you have. Numbers go from mere visitors to prospects on your email lists who in turn make purchases. Traffic is vital to your online marketing strategy and commercial goals. Without it, you don't get to close sales, you don't get to succeed in every other thing that is required for sustainability.

Filling up your sales funnel.

The more people fill up the top of the tunnel, the more sales you experience below where the real buyers of your products are. The longer a person stays on your site, probing around a product, the more likely he'll make a purchase.

Traffic helps you forecast the growth in your business.

You can tell how your business is doing by how many visitors come to your website. The projection is simple. Not all traffic is good, while some bog down your website, others are beneficial. Once you can measure the number of beneficial traffic, you find out how to optimize for your business. (More on optimizing in the next chapter.)

You are doing something right.

Especially if you are getting the right kind of traffic, it means your SEO writing is on point, it means your product copy is converting as it should and it also means the website is truly ranking. Generally, your website doesn't just go up on the list of search results, you have to be actively working to make that happen, so if it is happening, you are getting it right.

Gives you a hint on brand perception.

Every brand owner wants to know how their brand is doing with the public, they are curious about how visitors perceive their brand. Traffic is the answer. Both organic traffic—resulting from non-paid on paid ads—and nonorganic traffic demonstrates whether your audience loves what you do or not. You can tell this from the comments visitors leave on your blog posts, or the feedback they leave on your ads.

WAYS TO GENERATE TRAFFIC ON YOUR WEBSITE.

There are many ways to generate traffic to your website, let's begin from the simplest:

Keyword research: Content is how you bring traffic your way. But you won't just dump content on your website and hope that it would automatically bring traffic just by occupying space on your site. Your content has to be written deliberately and utilizes keywords that make it stick out in search results. When people search for data in your niche or genre, they use specific words, know those words, and use them when writing blog posts for your website. Websites like Moz, Ahrefs, and SEMrush are tools that help you understand what keywords your competition is using and how often people search the internet for your products using specific keywords. You are not going to be indiscriminately dumping these keywords in your articles or blog posts. They have to be in strategic places of your posts; the page title, meta description, headers, or the URL.

Create great content: I can't say this enough: content is king. Invest in creating wow content; they have to be informative, they have to give value, and they have to be memorable. Traffic is people prowling the internet for solutions to their problems, answers to their questions. If your content gives this value, your traffic will convert quickly and continue to do so. Lack of consistency kills traffic, so be sure to schedule posting great content; twice a week or four times a month. Your writing should be thorough, the answers should be specific and accurate. Let your stats guide your frequency, too; note what sort of content resonates more with your audience. If a particular post is drawing massive clicks, find out what is causing this traffic and double on it. Post well-researched content regularly, and your traffic will improve.

Active social media pages: Do you have social media pages? Millions of your target audience are on social media. Social places like Facebook offer means of interaction like Facebook pages. Many brands grow their following on this page. Social media pages are awesome for pulling crowds to your website. Its relaxed aura and playful milieu are ideal for introducing your brand to the target audience. Post your contents, eBooks, promotions with links that drive traffic from there to your website. One of the reasons social media pages are a great way to build your brand while attracting traffic is the reactions and comments. Social media pages create extremely apparent metrics for observing how your brand is perceived by the public. You can tell how a blog post is doing by the reactions and comments on the page and build on the success you see.

You can interact with your audience on each specific post by replying to them in real-time, hashtags helps to spread the word on a specific theme, you can update links on your profile to assist your audience track new products, you can change your profile photos to reflect whatever is going on with your brand at any given time. It is a whole world of traffic movement on social media.

Traffic through paid ads: An efficient way to drive traffic to your website is through paid search, social media, and display ads. These ads appear in searches on the internet; people click and are directed to your website. Paid ads are based on keywords search. Sometimes your keyword may not do well as you expect, or users may block ads on their browsers, which means your ads become invisible to a section of your audience irritated by ads. Although paid ads are a great way to drive traffic, they have their downsides, and you may have to consider if you are going to invest in them. The average cost per click ranges from $1 to $2 for Google ads. Concentrate on the keywords you want to target the most, so your budget is put to best use.

Emails and Newsletters: Mobile-friendly emails are also a great way to drive traffic to your web business. As we have noted earlier, 46% of emails are opened on mobile, so personalize your emails by addressing the recipient with their names, use an attractive template to spread them more quickly. Include a few lines from your blog post in the body of the mail, a link or button that redirects the subscriber back to the main content on your website. Include share buttons so the content can easily be shared on social media and with friends.

Publish guest posts on authoritative websites in your niche: Create content that contributes to progress in your chosen industry and publish it as a guest post on a traditional blog in your place. It could be articles exposing new research in your industry or develop tools that provide solutions to problems peculiar to your industry. Doing this drives massive traffic to your website. Doing this sets you up as an authority to reckon with; your audience is more quickly converted to leads boosting your sales. In addition to generating more traffic, you would be getting a valuable backlink for your site.

Attractive Headlines: Master the beautiful art of writing compelling headlines for your blog posts. Internet users have about a few seconds to spare each item on their screen. To hook them, your headline has to be catchy, thought-provoking. They have to pique curiosity and draw the reader in at first glance. If you are writing your content yourself, check out how popular websites do it. Buzzfeed is one of the websites with the best headlines on the internet today. They reportedly wrote up to twenty different headlines for a post before choosing one of them. That is how seriously these websites consider writing a great headline. With the right font and shade, your headline can either shine as a beacon or be as ineffectual as an unpainted wall.

SEO: What's traffic without SEO? Search Engine Optimization helps your traffic in ways that would blow your mind. So much has been written about SEO, yet websites continue to underutilize it. Invest your time on on-page SEO, off-page SEO, and technical SEO and experience a traffic surge on your website.

Add videos to your content: For most Internet users' visual information is more engaged than text, and retention is higher. Video marketing is an excellent tool that you can't afford to overlook.

Mind your competition: "We don't care what others are doing; we just focus on doing our own thing" We've heard people say those words or something close. You can't afford to be oblivious to your competition's moves or what they're doing. Your competitor probably checks on you and is trying to beat you all the time. And they probably are winning. If you haven't used the tool, BuzzSumo to check what your competitors are doing, then you are wrong. This tool aggregates what users on the internet are reading, what sites they're reading them, and what topics are resonating with them at given times. You can also find out what topic is trending on social media. Imagine what great content you can contribute to this content pool and how much traffic can come to your website.

The work to keep your website hydrated, so to speak, doesn't stop with generating traffic. Of course, traffic can become almost automated after a while, but you sure know things peak out after a while as well, which is why in the next chapter, we will examine how you can keep tabs on what's happening from your end.

MEASURING AND OPTIMIZING

An example of the growing child.

Most of us have a wall in the corner of the home where we checked our heights when we were kids. Our moms would have us stand against that wall, and she'd mark a point on the wall with a marker to show how tall we had gotten from the last time. She'd make sweet remarks about how tall we've grown over the previous two days or how she was going to add more veggies, vitamins, or proteins to our meals to help us grow taller.

Websites have tools that enable them to do something much like this. A lot of work goes into building an online business, it is not all rosy as some think, and the traffic and sales don't just begin to pour in or continue to do so without effort from the owner of the business. Consider some of the reasons it is essential to measure how your website is doing to take steps to optimize.

WHY MEASURE AND OPTIMIZE?

You optimize for the sake of your visitors. After doing all the work, traffic to the website increases, and leads begin to multiply. The more prospects derive value from your website, the more the need arises to measure how many visitors you get, how much of them become leads, and how this has affected sales. The difference tells you if you need to optimize. And you usually have to because the value of your content reaches a peak when you notice a dwindling in leads. You know, if your visitors must continue to get value, you have to know what they're up to. So you do it for the community of your fans.

You optimize for your business.

An optimized website becomes more effective for your business. You are in business to provide value, but you are not really in the humanitarian business even though you give free stuff. Your company pays itself and you. For your business to continue to grow, you must always measure how well it's doing in sales, and trust me, you will always need to optimize for more growth.

But what exactly are you optimizing?

What reason the website ABC optimizes for will be different from what website XYZ does it for. Optimizing your website depends on the focus of the site.

When people visit my website, what are they searching for? Are they looking to purchase a product? If so, optimize your site so they can find the products more efficiently. Are they searching for suggestions on self-help books? Optimize so that your website can help them achieve that task more efficiently.

You optimize for your business goals.

Your visitors' goals are closely linked with those of your business. The visitors who click on your website are attracted by the synchronicity of purpose. What's the KPI (Key Performance Indicator) of your business? When you know the answer to this question, you know exactly what to test and fix to optimize your website.

Here are a few things to optimize on your website

Optimize Landing Pages

Optimize your landing pages as this is the first page visitors find themselves when they interact with your business. If visitors keep getting bounced off the landing page, they may get tired and assume you don't want them on your website.

You can tell how efficiently your landing pages work by checking on your analytics.

Optimize Conversion Boxes

Conversion boxes are also a vital place to check for optimization. If you check your analysis and discover that 200 people visited the box requesting visitors to sign up for a three-day trial, but only 50 got to sign up, then you know that page needs optimizing as well. This may be why leads are low in your business. Instead of reinforcing ads, optimizing may be all your need to boost sales again.

Optimize Checkout Page

For a website that sells products, visitors are often directed to the checkout page. After filling out products and the buyer can't check out the product, they may get tired and move to another website. Noticing this trend on your website can be an opportunity to optimize.

Optimize About Us Page

This is a crucial page for your business. Prospects visiting your site would want to know more about your business. Your prospects are more inclined to take action when your about us page gives off a trustworthy atmosphere

Here are some of the best website optimization tools that help you *evaluate* the success of your website:

Google Analytics

This is perhaps the most helpful tool Google has ever made for free. Google Analytics is a tool that tracks how well your website can accomplish that which you built it for. Note that if you are using this tool for the first time, it will not show you how your website has been doing in the past. It doesn't work retroactively. Google Analytics shows you how many people visit your website. If not many people find your website and you are not aware of this, you may not know what to do to remedy the situation. This is one of the things this tool does for you. It tells you the number of visitors and the number of times each one visits. It shows how people find your website; organic search, direct search, from social media, or by referrals. Since many websites have a target audience, like those who sell particular kinds of products, google analytics helps you know who's visiting and whether these visitors are in the bracket of people who would buy from you. Google also released a Heatmap that gives you a graphical representation of your site's data. The Heatmap helps you see how visitors engage with your website, the links they click on, and the parts of your page they are most interested in. Having all this information helps you determine if your website is accomplishing its purpose.

Google Analytics does a lot more. If you aren't using it, it's time to do so.

Kissmetrics

This tool reports on people who come to your site. While Google Analytics tells you *what's* happening on your site, this tool tells you *who's* responsible for the actions. With this tool, you can better spot valuable visitors, the parts of your site with the highest conversion rates. This tool compliments Google Analytics well.

Crazyegg

Great tool here, very page specific. It is a heat mapping tool that shows where users click on your pages and how far down they scroll on a page on your website. This tool helps you know if things like the email request box are too far down the page and you have to optimize. Or if the structure of your articles tires out your visitors because they have to scroll too often. Again, great tool.

Unbounce

This is a landing page testing tool that helps create and test different variations of your landing page. It is also an excellent tool for businesses that frequently run paid advertising campaigns.

VWO *(Visual Website Optimizer)*

These tool tests variations you toggle around your web elements like copy, images, and CTA buttons. It aims to let you see which variations help your website work better.

13

THE IMPORTANCE OF GOING FAST

The Example of Cowboy Cricket Farms.

In 2016, Kathy Rolin of Belgrade Montana told her husband she wanted to start a cricket farm. By January 2017, they had started breeding crickets in large quantities. Soon they were getting so many orders that they could hardly keep up, and they had to shut down orders because of the avalanche that was pouring in. To respond to the high demand for their product, they created a network of partners around the country. Now they have more than 12 partners. What some companies achieved in decades, Kathy and her husband did within two years. They did have the help of a mentor Rick Sanders who volunteers with Bozeman SCORE, who helped them develop the couple's business plan.

Kathy Rolin had an idea and went all out to make it work. She didn't wait until the world was perfect.

DON'T WAIT FOR THE GRASS TO GROW.

How many of us had glorious dreams of seeing our business shoot to the moon overnight? We've all been there. Overnight success only ever happens in the movies. People often talk about the patient's dog, that he ate a fat bone. You wonder where the fat bone came from. Someone must have at least dropped the bone. The point is effort must be expended in making success happen. If you have an idea and just enough material to launch it, go ahead and do it. Like Kathy and her husband, all they needed to do was bring together crickets and breed on a patch of land that was already theirs in a state known for rearing cattle. If you have an idea for a website to solve some human problem, by all means, learn what it requires to launch it, establish your brand and begin to grow.

TIPS TO GROW FAST.

Have a timeline for growth.

Design a projection for your business. It is not too early in the game for you to plan where you want your business to be in the next five years. Have projections for every phase of the business growth.

Employ the right people.

With the right people in your corner, your growth is accelerated. Kathy Rolin had the help of a mentor, which propelled their business faster than anyone imagined. Having a team that shares the same passion for growth with you is invaluable for development.

Avoid taking unnecessary risks.

You can't control everything around you, and circumstances beyond your control may afflict your business along the way. But it is essential to limit such occurrences by avoiding people or situations that may predispose your digital business to fraud, theft of your records or business plan, or ideas. If your business requires storage, insure such property. Do not be too quick to add people to your staff or to rent more office space.

Be flexible and adaptable.

A rigid plan leaves no room for change in circumstances. A new business that lacks adaptability grinds to a stop when unanticipated changes occur. But you don't have to pack up when overwhelmed by either a growing demand for your web resources or when the market seems not in your favor. By being flexible, you quickly discover what works and what doesn't; you discover legitimate shortcuts to solving supply issues. When the demand for crickets went off the roof, Kathy Rolin solved the problem by creating a network of "partner farmers." You'll find that there is always a way around any obstacle to your startup, and you'd move fast.

Latch on to customer experience.

Hold fast to giving your customers value and more than their money's worth, and they'll become your biggest advertisers. Instead of focusing on profit and expansion, let your product do the talking and traveling. If your product is excellent, your customers will talk about it and if not, brace yourself.

Reinvest in the business.

It is a startup; treat it as one. At first, your profits would come in trickles. Resist the urge to keep it all. Put the profits back into the business and plug it into any company areas in need of more attention. If you now need to hire more hands to increase production, do it. If the demand for your products increases and you need more hands, then get them.

Be proactive.

Be ready to project into the future, develop the ability to see around the corner of situations. Suppose there's a vacant apartment downstairs, a cheap one; you may want to lease it because considering your sales sheet from the past two months, you might need more room in the coming few weeks. Room for what? Perhaps, storage, office space, or even an assembly point or a packaging place for your deliveries.

Give your customers premium treatment. Work on consistently exceeding customer expectations. They'll share their experiences with others; this way, your web business benefits from referrals.

Be interested in your competition.

This does not mean rivalry. Your competition can be one of your most excellent teachers as a startup. For one thing, your competition was most likely in the business before you. Knowing what they did or didn't do from research can help you avoid all the mistakes they made. You might even learn to do it better than them.

Growth is everything in business, whether it be fast or slow. A stagnant business is likely not making sales and would probably pack up sooner. Aim for rapid growth because if you don't, your competition will. You have to think on your feet. And this is the sense of this chapter. If you have a business idea, run it. If you are going to launch it, do it fast. And when you do, expect that competitors will crawl out of the woodwork trying to beat you. Trust that your idea will be copied, which is why you have to aim for fast growth in your business.

Conversely, you must be careful *how* you move. In the next chapter, learn how to take things slow while moving.

THEN GO SLOW AND STEADY

An Example: Wise Acre Frozen Treats.

His name was Jim Picariello. He started the company named Wise Acre Frozen Treats, selling organic popsicles in a schoolhouse kitchen in 2006. After a year and a half, he hired a single employee, which wasn't bad. But six months passed, and he hired more. This time, 13 more employees entered a large manufacturing facility. Later that year, the company went bankrupt. Picariello's mistake was that he hired a big staff too soon. He didn't have the revenue or startup capital to pay for those investments.

Picariello's is an example of a business that rose too fast. You can contrast this example with the one in the last chapter about Kathy Rolin and her husband. What do you learn as a web startup from these examples?

THE DANGERS OF GROWING TOO FAST.

You lose track of your expenditure.

One of the most common problems you will encounter in your business if you allow yourself to move too fast is losing your head regarding how much is coming in and going out of your financial pocket. In the beginning, you can pretty much calculate off-hand or on paper how much money you're making and how much you spend in running the digital startup. But things change when you begin to tinker with such vast amounts as from $5 million. It is tricky. You tell yourself it's not time to hire an accountant to work for you full time, yet you can't seem to be able to do anything about your heavy finances. Not being able to keep track is the beginning of trouble.

Confusing cash flow.

This is another problem that is peculiar to small businesses. If a startup owner confuses his profits, money on hand after deducting expenses income, he sets himself up for trouble.

Focusing too much on sales.

When your business grows too fast, you begin to think that as long as your digital product is selling, you can invest in an expansion. But in reality, sales isn't the only factor that determines if you are ready to hire more employees, rent more offices, and so on.

Hiring the wrong people.

This can happen to your business when you are in a hurry to grow. You probably have loans to pay back, or you have huge orders coming in, and things are looking great that you relax on qualifications for hiring people. But this, too, is a trap that businesses that grow too fast fall into.

Mistakes with management.

This is something that almost always happens with startups that are growing too fast. You lose your head in the day-to-day running of the business, and you lose sight of the essential parts of the business. Overworked employees. Rushed growth takes a toll on your team members or employees. You push them so much, and they don't probably get paid for their work. Or because you push your employees too hard, make them work insane hours, they then keep leaving, you keep hiring new ones. This affects your productivity and even customer care.

Finally, pressure cripples your ability to lead. It doesn't take time before you lose touch. You are overworked; your employees are overworked. This fatigue soon begins to reflect in the way business is run.

Moving too fast almost always kills the entire operation. Instead of aiming to achieve fast success, it is best to move slow but steady. Do not confuse being ready to begin a business and launching it with what you have, where you are, with starting a business and trying to expand too fast. They are two different things.

There is being ready to handle expansion and just rushing from being a startup into hiring more than your web business can cater to. A startup can maintain its size and still be fast in achieving the status of a well-known brand. A startup that moves too fast may not even have achieved the status that allows it to be a brand to reckon with. Such a startup dies even before it reaches its purpose.

15

BUILD A STRONG COMMUNITY

The Example of Harley Davidson.

In 1983, Harley Davidson was in dire straits financially. Profitability was low, overhead was killing operations. It seemed like there was no way out. But 25 years later, in 2009, the company was valued at $7.8 billion. They did it by investing in their brand community and improving the loyalty of their customers. This enthusiastic group of brand advocates was encouraged to live the lifestyle that the brand represented. Then they used these ambassadors to spread the word about their brand.

This wasn't easy, but the advantages years later far outweigh the difficulties of achieving it.

BENEFITS OF BUILDING A COMMUNITY.

Building a community around your customers gives you insight into how they perceive your product. And it helps your business incorporate what they learn into upgrades that answer the very desire of your customers. There is a symbiosis between business goals and customer satisfaction. There is no higher dream like having a community of customers that live for your web products.

With a community of customers, you enjoy their trust. Because they trust you, they don't go on Google to leave bad reviews upon experiencing a defect in your web products. The reviews or feedback they leave for your products reflect a community of people who value their brand relationship.

Your community is your brand advocate. They root for your business. They set up forums of a community of users and invite people to join them, all of this without your input most times.

Many of your customers will treat your community as a support channel other than your business offers on your website. For example, we have support channels independent of the company itself on social media like Facebook and Linkedin groups. You can have professionals coming together in such channels to provide solutions to customer grievances about products.

HOW TO BUILD COMMUNITIES AROUND YOUR BUSINESS.

Be customer-focused.

Have a customer-centric approach to your product. Make products that inspire your customers. It is easier to build a community around a product that customers love. Even if the number of your customers is few, it is a springboard for an expanding community.

Let your product encourage users to meet each other. If your product is the sort that encourages users to meet, then you stand a better chance at building a community around it. A web design company is a proper fit too. Your product is such that friends can use and compare notes on utility and are quick to exchange tips on dealing with issues enablesyour product might have.

Give your customers a share of the work.

Make them feel like their input is important to any upgrade or new products you have coming out. It means that at the early stage of building your community, you have to engage them without interfering in the relationship between your users. Respond to feedback, answer their questions and let this feedback reflect in the product you release.

Be approachable.

As the CEO of your company, if you are easy to talk to, your company will also be. If your employees are afraid to speak to you, it is not likely that people in your customer community will be able to approach you. It translates easily, approachability that is. Your customers have to see you interact with them regularly on the platform.

Show up physically.

Organize a meetup where your community of customers attends. It could be a workshop where you talk to them about your products, a new one that's coming, or a new way to use an old product. At such a meeting, members of your community have the chance to interact not just with you but also with one another.

Consider having a platform.

Having a platform is an excellent idea for meeting with your community online. It can be on LinkedIn, Facebook, or some other medium. There are no complex rules on your platform as long as you are close to your customers.

In 2008, Lego launched the Lego Ideas Platform, which allowed fans to submit new concepts for Lego sets. The winner of the contest was given 1% of the royalties when the set was produced. The community has grown to over a million users since. And the Lego company is the biggest toy company today. This is how powerful a community is for a brand. The benefits can not be quantified in money terms. The community is not just a group of users but a family of people who love your product and who enjoy using it. Community building is a process; it takes time to find people among your users who are passionate about the product. When you see them, involve them in the product mechanism of your company. Focus on their passion. You want to know what they'd do to your product if given a chance. You'd be surprised what you find. Having communities for your development is a fun way to grow your business. So as a web startup, never underestimate what life your customers can bring to your business.

Building an eight-figure website is a journey that you do not rush. But as you work your way up, it may get more challenging, but you learn. You will have to reinvent yourself, in your customer interaction especially, to stay in business.

Listening and implementing feedback from your customers will help cement your relationship with a solid customer base. Many new businesses have found that one of the best ways to stay connected to your community is by creating a culture of care. This is perhaps why it is called customer care. And this is the whole essence of business in the first place, to provide value to your customers. It is human nature to be drawn to people who care about us. Your community of users will stay if they sense this care

Printed in Great Britain
by Amazon